GREAT GIFTS™

TOAST THE HOST

Copyright © 1996 Cy DeCosse Incorporated 5900 Green Oak Drive Minnetonka, Minnesota 55343
1-800-328-3895 All rights reserved Printed in U.S.A.

Library of Congress Cataloging-in-Publication Data Toast the host. p. cm. ISBN 0-86573-988-9 1. Handicraft. 2. Gifts. 3.
Gift wrapping. I. Cy DeCosse Incorporated.   TT157.T57 1996 745.5 — dc20 96-15851 CIP

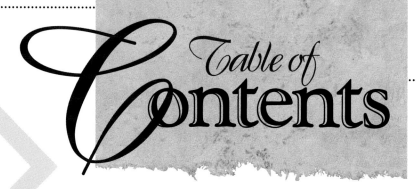

Table of Contents

Flower & Plant Presentations *4-7*

Gifts of Crystal & Glass *8-9*

Napkin Rings *10-13*

Table Linen Bouquets *14-17*

Dinner Bells *18-19*

Votive Candles *20-23*

◀ Bobèches *24-27*

Festive Fruits & Nuts *28-31*

Potluck Gifts *32-33*

Candy & Snack Presentations *34-37*

Birch-log Gifts *38-39*

Wine-bottle Bags & Containers *40-43*

Hot Mulled Drinks *44-47*

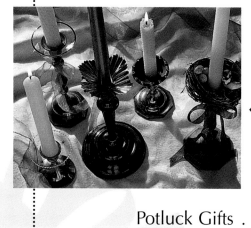

Homemade Coasters 48–51

Books as Gifts 52–53

Personalized Stationery 54–57

Customized Music Tapes . . . . . 58–61 ▶

Day-after Party Gift 62–63

Breakfast Easter Basket 64–67

The Bread Basket 68–71

Gifts of Silver 72–73

Seasonal Wreaths & Swags 74–79

Holiday Decor Starter Kit 80–81

New Homeowner Gifts 82–85

Springtime Gardener Gifts 86–87

Outdoor Survival Kits 88–89

Stovetop Potpourri . . . . 90–93 ▶

Flower & plant
PRESENTATIONS

Flowers and plants are always popular as host or hostess gifts. Creative containers enhance their presentation and become an extra gift. For example, select an attractive container, such as a vintage ceramic pitcher, antique tin, glass milk bottle, or enameled teapot. If desired, protect containers with plastic pot liners, available at craft or floral stores. Trim the containers with ribbon or raffia.

Learn how to keep cut flowers from your garden fresh, then wrap them in colorful tissue and cellophane. Do not overlook the possibility of giving a dried arrangement, either. Dried flowers will last for a year or two if kept out of direct sunlight and can be presented in the same ways as fresh flowers.

Tips for Keeping Flowers Fresh

☞ *Cut the stems of most fresh flowers at an angle, using a sharp knife, to increase water absorption. Snap stems of chrysanthemums.*

☞ *Cut stems of roses under water at an angle, 1" to 2" (2.5 to 5 cm) from the end, using a sharp knife. If stems are not cut under water, air bubbles form at the ends of stems, preventing water from rising up the stems.*

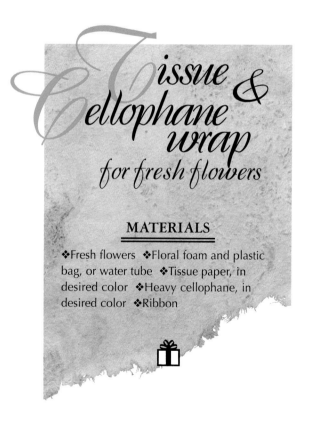

Tissue & Cellophane wrap for fresh flowers

MATERIALS

❖Fresh flowers ❖Floral foam and plastic bag, or water tube ❖Tissue paper, in desired color ❖Heavy cellophane, in desired color ❖Ribbon

1 Trim stems of fresh flowers and insert stems in floral foam or water tube, as directed above.

2 Cut tissue and cellophane into squares that measure across the diagonal $1\frac{1}{2}$ times the length of your flowers. (Tissue square may be slightly smaller than cellophane square, if desired.) Place cellophane on flat work surface; layer tissue over cellophane.

☞ *Place stems of cut flowers into a piece of floral foam that has been saturated with water; then cover the foam with a plastic bag. Secure with twist tie or string. Or insert stems in filled water tubes. Both floral foam and water tubes are available at floral or craft stores.*

☞ *Keep fresh flowers out of direct sunlight and drafts.*

☞ *Include a packet of cut-flower food, available at flower shops, with your fresh flower arrangement.*

☞ *Remove any leaves from the bottom portion of flower stems that will be covered by water.*

3 Place the flowers diagonally across tissue, with one corner of the tissue just showing at tops of the flowers. Fold bottom corner of tissue up over stems.

4 Gather the cellophane and tissue around the stems of the flowers just below blossoms. Secure with ribbon. Fluff top of the tissue, leaving the blossoms of the flowers exposed.

GIFTS *of* Crystal & glass

There are many lovely and affordable gift items made from crystal and glass available in housewares and gift stores. Depending on how well you know your gift recipient, you can purchase a small item or start a collection of goblets, barware, or figurines. Add to the collection as gift-giving occasions arise.

Single items include candlesticks, bowls, photo frames, vases, wine decanters, ornaments, or jewelry. Give candles with candlesticks and fill bowls with potpourri or colorfully wrapped hard candies. Fill vases with fresh flowers, or include a bottle of refill oil with glass oil lamps.

Napkin rings

Napkin rings are a perfect gift for people who entertain often, helping to add variety to their dinner parties. You can purchase inexpensive or extravagant napkin rings, or you can use simple materials and techniques to create your own style.

Curve old silverware into a circular form around a dowel or a pipe by tapping it with a wooden mallet. Assemble a collection of seasonal cookie cutters for use as napkin rings, embellishing them with ribbon, if desired. Bend artificial berry clusters with flexible wire stems into arches to clasp onto napkins. Or try the simple wire or rope styles shown on the following pages.

Couple your napkin rings with a set of napkins and a tablecloth or placemats. For classically styled napkin rings, select brocade napkins. Napkin rings fashioned from rope can be paired with bandannas.

Coiled wire Ring

MATERIALS

❖18-gauge copper wire ❖Dowel or pipe
❖Needlenose pliers

☞ *To prevent making impressions on wire with pliers, wrap masking tape around toothed grips of pliers.*

1 Cut wire into 2-yd. (1.85 m) length. Wrap piece of wire tightly around a dowel or pipe until it is completely coiled.

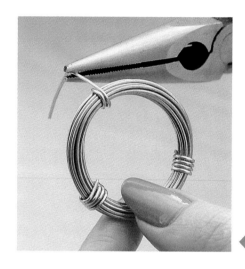

2 Cut three 2" (5 cm) lengths of wire. Wrap 2" (5 cm) lengths tightly around large coil of wire; evenly space short lengths around coil. Pinch ends of short wires with needlenose pliers to secure.

Spiral wire Ring

MATERIALS

❖14-gauge wire ❖³⁄₈" (1 cm) dowel ❖Pliers
❖Wide dowel or pipe ❖Needlenose pliers
❖Aerosol acrylic paint in
desired color,
optional

☞ *When wrapping wire around small dowel, it may be helpful to grasp wire with a rubber jar opener for a better grip.*

1 Cut wire into 1½-yd. (1.4 m) length. Wrap wire tightly around ³⁄₈" (1 cm) dowel to make spiral; remove spiral from dowel.

2 Slightly stretch spiraled wire by gently pulling ends apart with pliers. Wrap spiraled wire around a wide dowel or pipe to make large ring. Turn ends, and pinch with needlenose pliers. Apply aerosol acrylic paint, if desired.

1 Cut wire into 1-yd. (0.95 m) length. Place center of wire length on wide dowel or pipe; wrap each end of wire two times around dowel or pipe, creating four rows of wire.

MATERIALS

❖14-gauge wire ❖Dowel or pipe ❖Needlenose pliers ❖Aerosol acrylic paint in desired color, optional ❖Two glass beads or jewels ❖Hot glue gun and glue sticks

2 Bend ends of wire into tight spirals, using needlenose pliers. Bend spirals so they face out at top and bottom of napkin ring. Apply aerosol acrylic paint, if desired.

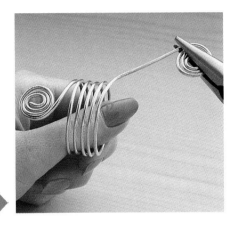

3 Secure glass beads to surface of tight spirals, using hot glue.

1 Cut the rope to at least 12" (30.5 cm) length. Unravel 3" (7.5 cm) on each end of rope.

Knotted rope Ring

MATERIALS

❖Heavy jute or sisal rope

2 Knot each piece of unraveled rope ends to unraveled pieces at opposite end. Fray ends of rope; trim ends, if necessary.

TABLE LINEN
Bouquets

There is a wide variety of decorative linens—towels, napkins, and placemats—available in most department stores and linen stores. They make excellent gifts that will get years of use. Many are seasonal or are printed with holiday patterns.

With a few basic folding techniques, you can combine colored and patterned linens to present "bouquets" of flowers. Select a floral-printed towel and surround it in a jar or vase with a second, solid green towel for "leaves." Or roll an assortment of linens to look like calla lilies, and arrange them in a ceramic pitcher. Coordinating napkins can be layered and stuffed into a large, round vase for a loose, leafy look.

Solid color Bouquet

MATERIALS

❖Four napkins of coordinating solid colors
❖Large round vase

1 Lay one napkin on flat surface. Layer remaining three napkins over the first, slightly offsetting each so no corners match up. ▼

2 Gather napkins together at the center creating a "bouquet." Insert "stem" end into vase. Fluff napkin corners to desired appearance.

Lily Bouquet

MATERIALS

❖At least 3 coordinating or matching linen towels ❖Vase or other container

1 Fold over short side of rectangular towel until towel is square, if necessary.

1 Fold floral napkin with an accordion fold. (If napkin is too long, fold in half first.)

MATERIALS

❖Floral-print napkin ❖Solid green napkin
❖Vase or other container

2 Fold green napkin in half, lengthwise. Fold in half, crosswise, at an angle so corners are slightly offset. Wrap green napkin around floral napkin so offset corners of green napkin are at top.

3 Insert bottom end in vase. Fan out floral napkin; fluff green napkin, and pull tips down to resemble "leaves."

2 Roll up square loosely from one corner to opposite corner. Insert one end in vase. Repeat with remaining towels.

3 Pull exposed ends of towels open and tips down so they resemble lilies.

Dinner bells

For a truly unique gift and conversation starter, give your host a dinner bell with which to call guests to the dinner table. Bells come in a variety of styles and sizes and really add a special touch to a formal table.

You can find new bells made from crystal, silver, brass, or ceramic for reasonable prices at department stores or gift stores. Or look in antique stores and at flea markets, where you'll find any number of interesting and vintage styles. Try to find a bell that will match your host's dinnerware or home decor.

Embellish bells with ribbons to suit their style. Silver and brass bells can be engraved at a jewelry or gift store. Rub-on transfers that resemble etching can be used on glass bells to personalize them.

To wrap the bell, stuff it with tissue to silence it; then wrap the entire bell up in several layers of tissue. Nestle the bell in a box or tie it up in a colorful fabric bag.

Votive CANDLES

Candles are very affordable and almost everyone likes to use them, so they are a practical and well-received gift. Votive candles are one of the most basic types of candle and the easiest to present decoratively.

Purchase several plain glass votive candle holders and a wide assortment of candles in a variety of colors, so you have them on hand for any occasion. With a few simple embellishments, such as ribbon, dried naturals, or garland, you can have lovely gifts on a moment's notice.

Ribbon Votive

MATERIALS

❖ Glass hurricane votive candle holder
❖ Wired ribbon

1 Cut ribbon 18" (46 cm) longer than circumference of base of candle holder. Wrap ribbon around base. Tie ribbon with bow. Trim ends of ribbon as desired.

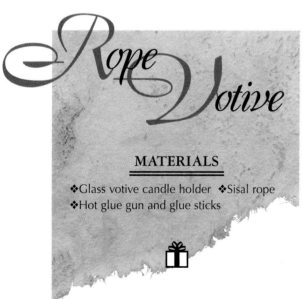

Rope Votive

MATERIALS

❖ Glass votive candle holder ❖ Sisal rope
❖ Hot glue gun and glue sticks

1 Secure the end of rope to side of candle holder at base, using hot glue.

2 Wrap rope around candle holder in a spiral from bottom to top, securing with hot glue as you wrap. Cover the entire candle holder in this manner.

3 Trim rope at top of candle holder at an angle; secure with hot glue.

1 Cut ribbon ½" (1.3 cm) longer than circumference of candle holder.

2 Secure one end of ribbon to side of candle holder, using hot glue. Wrap ribbon around candle holder, completely covering it with ribbon. Fold end of ribbon under for a clean edge; secure with hot glue.

3 Secure dried naturals around the base of candle holder, using hot glue. If naturals are too round or bulky, such as pinecones, cut them in half with craft scissors before securing to candle holder.

Dried naturals Votive

MATERIALS

❖Glass votive candle holder ❖Ribbon with width equal to candle holder height ❖Hot glue gun and glue sticks ❖Dried naturals, such as miniature pinecones or flowers

---

1 Wind garland once around base of candle holder, twisting end around itself to secure.

2 Wrap garland around candle holder in a spiral from bottom to top. Twist top end around itself to secure.

☞ *Colored glass candle holders are very pretty with this treatment.*

Star garland Votive

MATERIALS

❖Glass votive candle holder ❖Mylar® wired star garland

Bobèches

Bobèches (bo-besh) are always appreciated as a host or hostess gift, since they protect candle holders and table linens from the dripping wax of candles. Bobèches catch melted wax and offer a decorative touch to simple taper candles.

Plain glass bobèches are available in housewares and craft stores, and, for a more elegant look, vintage crystal bobèches from chandeliers are available at antique stores. You can make your own inexpensive bobèches from copper or tin sheets, terracotta saucers, or small, craft bird's nests, as shown on the following pages.

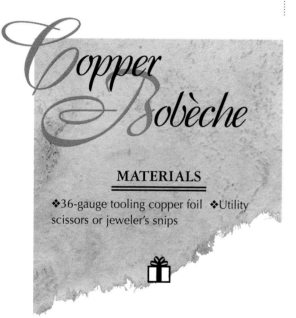

Copper Bobèche

MATERIALS

❖36-gauge tooling copper foil ❖Utility scissors or jeweler's snips

1 Cut a 3" (7.5 cm) square or a circle, 3" (7.5 cm) in diameter, from metal sheet, using scissors or snips. Fold metal piece in half; fold in half again in opposite direction.

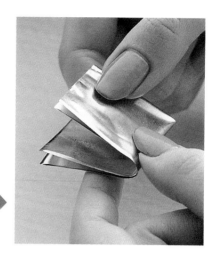

2 Cut a ½" (1.3 cm) semi-circle at folded corner of metal piece to create a hole in the center.

3 Unfold metal piece; check to make sure it slides over a taper candle. Trim as necessary.

☞ *Use pinking shears to trim around bobèche for a jagged edge.*

☞ *Fold slight creases uniformly around bobèche, if desired.*

☞ *For an antique verdigris finish on copper, apply chemical solution for creating verdigris finish to copper following manufacturer's directions.*

1 Cut hole in center of nest so it fits snugly around taper candle.

2 Secure desired embellishments to the nest, using hot glue.

MATERIALS

❖Craft bird's nest, available at craft stores
❖Desired embellishments, such as ribbons, craft eggs, or a small craft bird
❖Hot glue gun and glue sticks

---

1 Soak the saucer in warm water for $1/2$ hour to soften it. Place saucer upside down on piece of scrap wood. With light but even pressure, drill hole in center of saucer bottom, using $3/4$" drill bit.

2 Gently file rough edges of hole, using rounded-edge file.

3 Embellish pot or saucer as desired, using paint or jewels secured with hot glue or craft glue.

Terra-cotta Bobèche

MATERIALS

❖Terra-cotta saucer with $2^{1}/2$" (6.5 cm) diameter ❖Drill and $3/4$" spade bit or ceramic drill bit ❖Scrap wood ❖Rounded-edge file ❖Desired embellishments, such as acrylic paint or imitation jewels or beads

FESTIVE
Fruits
& nuts

Nuts and dried fruit are nice gifts with a country feel. You can put together collections of nuts in the shell, seasoned mixed nuts, or jars of colorful dried fruit. Flavorful trail mixes combining fruits and nuts are easy to make, too.

Layer dried fruits, such as apricots, cherries, cranberries, apples, and figs, in vintage canning jars; tie a country-style ribbon around the top of the jar. Small shelled nuts and seeds, like pistachios, sunflower seeds, and pumpkin seeds, work well with this treatment, too.

Fill large penny-candy jars with two colors of pistachio nuts; tie a bow around the neck of the jar. Trail mixes and seasoned nuts can be placed in plastic wrap or foil-lined vintage tins. Or fill an unglazed terra-cotta pot with nuts, and cover it with the inverted saucer.

Terra-cotta Nut pot

MATERIALS

❖Terra-cotta pot and saucer with equal diameters ❖Mixed nuts in the shell, such as walnuts, Brazil nuts, pecans, almonds, and hazelnuts ❖Raffia ❖Screw eyes ❖Drill and ¹/₁₆" drill bit, if necessary

1 Fill pot with mixed nuts. Invert saucer over pot to cover nuts. Secure saucer in place by tying raffia from bottom of pot to top of saucer, knotting at top.

2 Twist screw eyes into ends of two or three nuts; predrill holes, if necessary. Tie raffia through screw eye, then to raffia at top of pot, allowing nuts to hang down side of pot.

☞ *If drilling holes in nuts, secure nuts in a vise grip first, or hold them with pliers.*

☞ *Place a nutcracker and nut picks under raffia at top of pot, or place them inside pot with nuts.*

Spicy Mixed Nuts

- ❖ 1/2 teaspoon (3 mL) ground cumin
- ❖ 1/2 teaspoon (3 mL) chili powder
- ❖ 1/2 teaspoon (3 mL) garlic salt
- ❖ 1/4 teaspoon (1 mL) cayenne pepper
- ❖ 1/4 teaspoon (1 mL) ground cinnamon
- ❖ 2 tablespoons (30 mL) olive oil
- ❖ 1 cup (250 mL) whole almonds
- ❖ 1 cup (250 mL) pecan halves
- ❖ Kosher salt

1 Heat oven to 325°F (160°C). In a small bowl, combine cumin, chili powder, garlic salt, cayenne, and cinnamon. Heat oil in small nonstick skillet over medium-low heat. Stir in spice mixture. Cook for 3 minutes, stirring frequently.

2 Combine almonds, pecan halves, and spice mixture in medium mixing bowl. Toss to combine. Spread nuts in single layer on large baking sheet. Bake for 12 to 15 minutes, or until lightly browned, stirring occasionally. Sprinkle with kosher salt. Allow to cool. Store in airtight container in cool place.

Makes 2 cups (500 mL)

Trail Mix

- ❖ 2 cups (500 mL) raisins
- ❖ 1 cup (250 mL) flaked unsweetened coconut
- ❖ 1 cup (250 mL) coarsely chopped dried apples
- ❖ 1/2 cup (125 mL) shelled sunflower seeds
- ❖ 1/2 cup (125 mL) shelled pumpkin seeds
- ❖ 1/2 cup (125 mL) whole cashews
- ❖ 1/2 cup (125 mL) whole almonds
- ❖ 1/2 cup (125 mL) dried cherries or cranberries

Combine all ingredients in a large bowl or sealable plastic bag. Store in an airtight container in a cool, dry place.

Makes 6 1/2 cups (1.6 L)

idea

Potluck
GIFTS

Often, you as a guest may be asked to bring a hot or cold dish to a potluck party. Make the container in which you bring your food the host or hostess gift; then you don't have to remember to take it home. A gift tag attached to the container or a personalized container makes this clear.

Salads can be presented in colorful acrylic or ceramic bowls or platters. Add color to the presentation by garnishing the salad with purple kale, fresh herbs, cherry tomatoes, or slices of fresh citrus fruit.

Decorative ovenproof casseroles with insulated or wicker carriers are perfect for hot dishes. Or include a set of hot pads or a trivet with the dish. Finally, take drinks in decorative bottles or pitchers. Insulated dispensers are great for hot drinks.

Candy & snack PRESENTATIONS

Since food is such a delightful and easy gift to give, you may be looking for new and interesting ways in which to present your homemade or specially purchased treats.

Ready-made containers include vintage tins lined with paper doilies or parchment paper and tied with ribbon. Line a small apple basket or galvanized pail with a country-style napkin, and fill it with caramel popcorn or assorted whole fruit. Fill a vintage colander with a party snack mix tied up in a cheesecloth or muslin bundle.

You can easily embellish plain pine boxes or even Chinese carry-out boxes, available at craft stores, and then fill them with candies. Ribbons and colorful napkins add a nice touch to any candy or snack presentation.

Painted Pine box

MATERIALS

❖Plain pine box ❖Aerosol acrylic paint in desired color ❖Shredded paper ❖Wrapped candy ❖Ribbon

☞ *Apply different colors of paint to lid and base of box.*

1 Apply aerosol acrylic paint to exterior of lid and base of box. Allow to dry.

2 Line bottom of box with shredded paper. Fill box with candy. Tie shut with ribbon.

Chinese Carry-out

MATERIALS

❖Plain Chinese carry-out box ❖Paint pens in desired colors ❖Pressure-sensitive tape ❖Metal beads or jewels ❖Hot glue gun and glue sticks

1 Make desired designs on box, using paint pens. Create a border along edges of painted design, using strips of pressure-sensitive tape.

2 Secure beads or jewels to the box as desired, using hot glue. Fill the box with candy.

Dipped-pretzel Bundles

MATERIALS

❖Dipped pretzel rods ❖Plastic wrap
❖Corrugated cardboard or heavy art paper
❖Twine, raffia, or ribbon

1 Wrap bundle of pretzel rods around the midsection with plastic wrap. Cut cardboard wide enough to conceal plastic wrap and long enough to overlap itself by 1" or 2" (2.5 or 5 cm). (If desired, wrap entire bundle of pretzels with plastic wrap.)

2 Wrap cardboard around bundle, concealing plastic wrap. Tie with twine, raffia, or ribbon.

☞ *To make dipped pretzel rods, melt almond bark (candy coating) as directed on package; dip pretzels in melted candy to cover 2/3 of each pretzel. Place on wax-paper-lined baking sheet; allow to dry. If desired, sprinkle pretzels with colored sugar before candy dries.*

Birch-log GIFTS

Birch logs are an idyllic way to bring warmth into a home. If you have easy access to fallen birch trees, use them to brighten others' homes.

In the wintertime, fill a flat basket with several pieces of birch logs. Add color sticks, pinecones, and long fireplace matches to the basket. Remove the matches from the box, tie them in a bundle with raffia, and attach the striking piece, which can be cut from the bottom of the matchbox.

Birch logs are terrific for summertime fireplaces, too. A bundle of three logs tied with raffia and embellished with sprigs of preserved cedar help to brighten unused fireplaces. Your gift recipient can save the bundle and use it year after year.

WINE-BOTTLE
Bags &
containers

Wine is a favorite host or hostess gift. Play on its popularity by making a special bag or container in which to present a bottle of wine.

Wine bags can be found in housewares and wine stores, or you can use basic sewing techniques and fabric scraps to make your own. Fabric netting and gold cord are ideal for dressing up a bottle of champagne. Or protect your bottle of wine by making a heavy paper tube and packing shredded paper around the bottle.

Attach a small book to the neck of the bottle or wine bag to use as a wine-tasting journal for the wine enthusiast. If the gift is for a close friend, plan to pass the wine bag and journal back and forth on gift-giving occasions, and keep track of the new wines the two of you try.

Felt Wine Bag

MATERIALS

❖ 2 pieces of felt fabric, cut to 15" × 9" (38 x 23 cm) ❖ Pinking shears ❖ Needle and thread, or sewing machine ❖ Ribbon or cording

☞ *To hang small book from ribbon, tie additional ribbon around length of inside of front cover and spine; tie to neck of bottle. Or drill a small hole in the top left corner of book, and thread ribbon through hole.*

1 Trim one short edge on each piece of fabric with pinking shears. These edges will be at the top of the bag.

2 Pin the fabric pieces right sides together. Stitch ¼" (6 mm) from raw edges along sides and bottom. Press seam allowances open. Turn bag right side out.

3 Fold top 3" (7.5 cm) of bag over. Cut sixteen ¼" (6 mm) vertical slits along fold at approximately 1" (2.5 cm) intervals. Unfold bag. Weave ribbon through slits; cinch bag closed, and tie ribbon with bow. If necessary, tie knots in ends of ribbon to prevent fraying.

Paper Wine Tube

MATERIALS

❖ Heavy corrugated paper ❖ Hot glue gun and glue sticks ❖ Shredded paper

1 Wrap paper around the bottle to determine size of piece needed. Cut to desired height, leaving part of bottle neck exposed; width should be equal to circumference of bottle plus ¾" (2 cm) for overlap.

1 Drill a small hole in one or both ends of the personalized tag. Set aside.

2 Spread netting on flat surface. Set bottle upright in center of netting. Gather netting around neck of bottle. Tie gold cording around neck of bottle; secure with a knot. Fluff top of netting.

3 Thread string through hole in brass tag; tie string around neck of bottle.

Netting with Engraved tag

MATERIALS

❖Personalized brass tag, available in jewelry or gift stores ❖Drill and ¹/₁₆" drill bit ❖36" (91.5 cm) square of fabric netting ❖Gold cording ❖Thin gold string

2 Wrap paper around bottle to form tube. Secure seam with hot glue. Remove bottle.

3 Cut square of paper so its sides equal the diameter of tube. Center tube on square. Bend corners of square up along side of tube; secure with hot glue. (Bend corners along a straightedge for cleaner edges, if desired.)

4 Place bottle in the tube. Stuff shredded paper into tube around neck of the bottle.

☞ *Use multicolored Mylar® strips instead of shredded paper for a festive look.*

HOT Mulled drinks

Hot mulled drinks, such as wassail, from an old Norse toast meaning "be in good health," are part of a tradition that goes back hundreds of years. These drinks are traditionally wine- or cider-based and are heated with spices, fruit, and sugar. They are sometimes fortified with rum or brandy.

Offer your autumn or winter party host a wish of good health by bringing the fixings for a hot, spirited drink to their gathering. You can arrange the ingredients in a decorative box or basket with instructions for preparing the drink. Include a set of mugs for serving their cup of cheer. If a more substantial gift is appropriate, place the ingredients in a special pot that can be used especially for the mulled drinks.

HOT MULLED DRINK RECIPES

☞ Wine, rum, or other liquids can be placed in decorative bottles, if desired.

☞ Spice mixes or brown sugar can be wrapped in a plastic wrap sachet and tied with ribbon, or sealed in a small plastic container.

Mulled Cider

❖ 1 small lemon
❖ 1 small orange
❖ 1/2 gallon (2 L) apple cider
❖ 4 sticks cinnamon, 3" (7.5 cm) long

❖ 1 cup (250 mL) dark rum or spiced rum
❖ 1/4 cup (50 mL) packed brown sugar

Assemble all ingredients in basket or box. Include the following instructions: Cut lemon and orange into slices. Combine cider, lemon and orange slices, and cinnamon sticks in saucepan or pot. Bring to a simmer over medium heat. (Do not boil.) Simmer for 15 minutes. Remove from heat. Stir in rum and sugar. Serve in mugs with slices of lemon or orange.

Mulled Wine

- 1 Tbs. (15 mL) packed brown sugar
- 1/4 tsp. (1 mL) ground nutmeg
- 1 to 3 whole allspice
- Cheesecloth; kitchen string
- 2 sticks cinnamon, 3" (7.5 cm) long
- 1 bottle (750 mL) dry red wine
- 1 pint (500 mL) port wine or brandy
- 1 large lemon studded with several whole cloves
- Additional cinnamon sticks, 3" (7.5 cm) long

1 Combine brown sugar, nutmeg and allspice in a double-layered cheesecloth sachet. Tie sachet with string; attach 2 sticks cinnamon to sachet with string. Assemble spice sachet and remaining ingredients in box or basket.

2 Include the following instructions: Combine all ingredients except additional cinnamon sticks in saucepan or pot. Bring to a simmer over medium heat. (Do not boil.) Simmer for 10 minutes. Serve in mugs with additional sticks of cinnamon.

Wassail

- 1/3 cup (75 mL) sugar
- 2 to 3 tsp. (10 to 15 mL) dried lemon peel
- 2 to 3 pieces candied ginger
- 1/2 tsp. (2 mL) ground allspice
- 1/4 tsp. (1 mL) ground nutmeg
- Cheesecloth; kitchen string
- 1 stick cinnamon, 3" (7.5 cm) long
- 1 orange
- 24 whole cloves
- 1 bottle (750 mL) dry red wine
- 3 cups (750 mL) apple cider

1 Combine sugar, lemon peel, ginger, cinnamon, allspice, and nutmeg in a double-layered cheesecloth sachet. Tie sachet with string; attach cinnamon stick to sachet with string. Assemble spice sachet and remaining ingredients in basket or box.

2 Include the following instructions: Cut unpeeled orange into 8 wedges. Stud each wedge with 3 cloves. Combine orange wedges, spice sachet, wine, and cider in saucepan or pot. Bring to a simmer over medium heat. (Do not boil.) Simmer for 15 minutes. Serve in mugs.

HOMEMADE
Coasters

Drink coasters are the perfect gift for someone who entertains a lot. They are essential for protecting furniture from the condensation that forms on glasses.

You can create a wide variety of whimsical coasters with simple, inexpensive materials, such as craft foam, rolled cork, corrugated plastic, or even rubber welcome mats. Cut these materials into initials, flowers, stars, or any design you desire for a customized look.

Craft foam Coaster

MATERIALS

❖Craft foam sheets in desired colors
❖Rubber cement, or hot glue gun and glue sticks ❖Craft scissors
❖Mat knife

1 Layer two sheets of foam in desired color pattern; secure, using rubber cement or hot glue.

2 Cut the desired shape of coaster out of layered foam, using craft scissors. Repeat for additional coasters.

3 Cut pieces of craft foam in desired shapes and colors for additional embellishments, using mat knife. For example, you may want to cut a piece in the same shape, but cut a hole in its center to let the piece under it show through. Secure pieces to the coaster, using rubber cement or hot glue.

Corrugated plastic Coaster

MATERIALS

❖Corrugated white plastic, such as Plasticor®, available at sign shops ❖Utility knife ❖Paint pens or permanent-ink markers in desired colors

1 Cut desired design out of plastic, using utility knife. If desired, use a cookie cutter, stencil, or pattern cut from scrap paper as a template and lightly trace design on plastic before cutting, using a pencil.

2 Embellish coaster as desired, using paint pens or permanent-ink markers.

1 Cut desired design out of floor mat, using mat knife.

Welcome-mat Coaster

MATERIALS

❖Rubber floor mat ❖Mat knife

☞ *Use this same method with artificial turf mats or carpet scraps.*

---

1 Unroll cork; flatten cork under books or other heavy objects for several hours.

2 Cut desired design from cork, using mat knife. If desired, use a cookie cutter, stencil, or pattern cut out of scrap paper as a template and lightly trace design on cork before cutting, using a pencil.

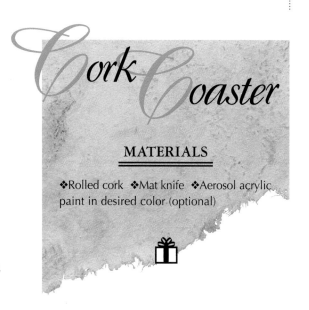

Cork Coaster

MATERIALS

❖Rolled cork ❖Mat knife ❖Aerosol acrylic paint in desired color (optional)

3 Paint coaster, using aerosol acrylic paint, if desired. Paint one or both sides of coaster, making sure edges are covered with paint.

Books *as* GIFTS

Books make wonderful gifts; since they are relatively inexpensive and cover such an infinite number of topics, you are sure to find one to suit the person destined to receive it.

Hobby-related books are a natural if you know someone who is an enthusiast. Books exist for the gardener, crafter, cook, antique buff, do-it-yourselfer, or collector of almost anything. Books on travel offer mental vacations or allow people to reminisce about places they've been. Popular books of fiction range from humorous cartoon books to the hottest-selling mystery.

Remember to inscribe a message on the inside cover of the book to add to its keepsake quality. Include an appropriate bookmark, such as a packet of seeds for the gardener or a piece of tapestry for the antique buff. You can even embellish a book on Hawaii with a lei, include packets of craft items with a craft book, or give a string of dried chilies with a book on the Southwest.

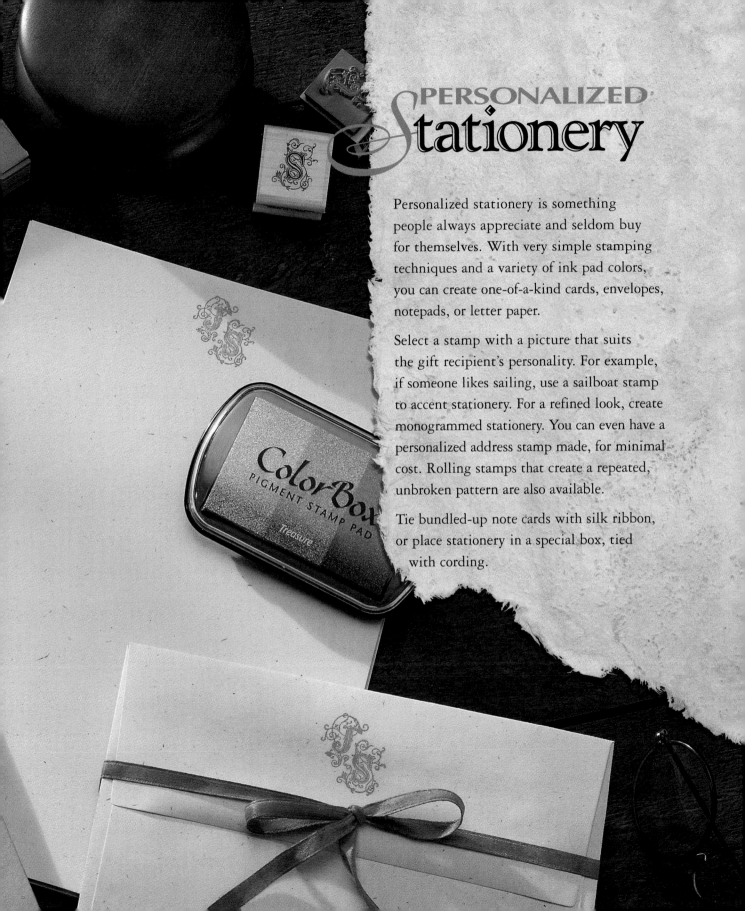

PERSONALIZED Stationery

Personalized stationery is something people always appreciate and seldom buy for themselves. With very simple stamping techniques and a variety of ink pad colors, you can create one-of-a-kind cards, envelopes, notepads, or letter paper.

Select a stamp with a picture that suits the gift recipient's personality. For example, if someone likes sailing, use a sailboat stamp to accent stationery. For a refined look, create monogrammed stationery. You can even have a personalized address stamp made, for minimal cost. Rolling stamps that create a repeated, unbroken pattern are also available.

Tie bundled-up note cards with silk ribbon, or place stationery in a special box, tied with cording.

Stamping techniques & tips

MATERIALS

❖Stamps ❖Ink pads ❖Blank note cards, envelopes, notepads, or loose paper

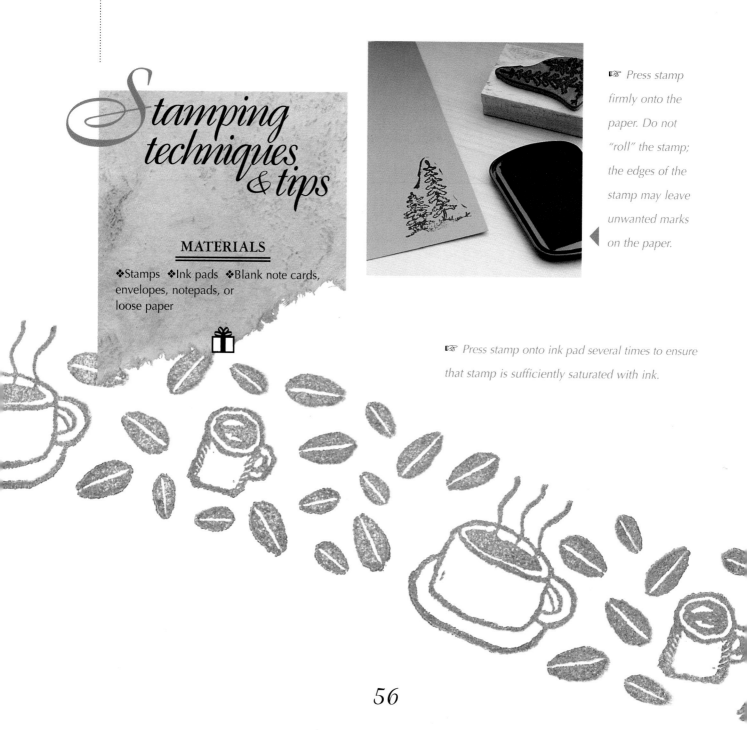

☞ Press stamp firmly onto the paper. Do not "roll" the stamp; the edges of the stamp may leave unwanted marks on the paper.

☞ Press stamp onto ink pad several times to ensure that stamp is sufficiently saturated with ink.

☞ *Practice your stamping and placement on a piece of scrap paper before stamping the stationery.*

☞ *Do not stamp shiny notecards, because the ink may smear.*

☞ *Multicolor and metallic ink pads, as well as solid colors, are available in craft or stationery stores.*

☞ *Use a clear plastic ruler as a guide when stamping, to ensure that patterns are uniform.*

CUSTOMIZED *Music* tapes

Create one-of-a-kind cassette tapes by custom-mixing music from your favorite records, tapes, or compact disks. Prepare a selection of party tunes, 50s or 60s classic rock, classical music, Christmas songs, jazz, or new age woodland music. Your gift recipient will appreciate the personal mix and the time that went into making it.

The presentation of your cassette tape should be as special as the music it contains. Make a decorative label and cover for the tape, using pictures, pressed flowers, ribbon, or drawings. Be sure to give a listing of the song names and artists in the tape case.

Cassette covers & Labels

MATERIALS

❖Case and jacket cover from blank cassette tape ❖Heavy art paper ❖Desired embellishments, such as ribbon, pressed flowers, photos, pictures cut from wrapping paper or magazines ❖Paper cement or craft glue ❖Transfer letters or acrylic paint for labels

1 Remove jacket cover from inside of cassette tape case. Use jacket as a template; trace outline on art paper. Cut outline from art paper.

2 Fold the art paper in the same manner as the original jacket cover, creasing folds with your fingers.

3 Decorate the jacket cover as desired, securing embellishments to the cover with paper cement or craft glue. Use transfer letters to create labels, or paint tape name on label, using a fine paintbrush.

☞ *While glue is drying in step 3, place sheet of wax paper over jacket cover, then weight it down with a heavy book. This will hold everything in place and prevent puckering.*

☞ *Decorate the cassette cover for a tape of 50s music with ad art cut from vintage magazines. Include a date or headline from a newspaper that indicates the era.*

☞ *Use a computer or typewriter to type labels and music lists. Cut labels and lists from paper; secure to label with paper cement or craft glue. Give white labels color by smearing an antique bronze or copper acrylic paint over lettering with your finger before cutting them out.*

☞ *Cut Christmas pictures from wrapping paper or cards for a tape of holiday music. Accent the label with gold ribbon.*

Day-after
PARTY GIFT

Take something really unique to the next party you attend. Give the host or hostess who always "goes all out" something they can really use: a recovery kit for the day after.

In a basket or gift box, package the following: bottled mineral water, antacid or pain relievers like acetaminophen or aspirin, flavored coffee or herbal tea, bubble bath, a tape or CD with soothing music, a gift certificate for home-delivery food or a package of soup mix, so your host doesn't have to cook, or a certificate for a maid service.

Stress Relief
MINERAL
BATH SALTS
SAMPLER

McGARV
The Best You C
McGarvey imports
quality 100% washes
from the premier
worldwide. The
coff   are e
and it mediat
our   special
in freshe
Enjoy

BREAKFAST
easter basket

A breakfast basket for Easter is a
lovely gift for a favorite couple,
be it their first Easter together or
their forty-first. Assemble all the
ingredients for a special breakfast
in a light-colored basket.

Use placemats to line the basket, and
roll up coordinating napkins to place
inside. For Eggs Benedict, assemble
eggs, Canadian-style bacon, English
muffins, and a hollandaise sauce mix.
For a lighter breakfast, fill the basket
with a variety of bagels and flavored
cream cheese. Add flavored coffees or
teas to baskets.

Decorated Easter eggs, Easter candy,
or a chocolate bunny help fill in the
gaps around the breakfast items. A
nice touch would be a romantic movie
video or a pair of movie tickets.

breakfast Easter Basket

MATERIALS

❖Basket ❖⁷/₈ yd. (0.8 m) fabric that frays easily, in pastel colors ❖Cotton batting ❖Colored paper Easter grass ❖Breakfast items ❖Fillers, such as Easter eggs and candy ❖Organdy or silk ribbons in pastel colors

1 Cut two 12" × 17" (30.5 × 43 cm) rectangles from fabric for placemats. Cut two 15" (38 cm) squares for napkins. Fray edges of fabric by removing several threads from the edges on all four sides of placemats and napkins.

2 Line basket with placemats. Cover bottom of basket with cotton batting. Cover batting with Easter grass to conceal it.

3 Roll napkins and insert them in one side of basket. Assemble breakfast items in basket so they are propped and any labels are visible. Fill spaces around large items with Easter eggs and candy.

4 Tie several ribbons around handle of basket.

☞ *Refrigerated items like Canadian bacon and fresh eggs should be kept cold until it is time to present the basket. Place fresh eggs in a small padded container to protect them from breakage.*

☞ *Purchased linen or paper napkins and placemats may be used instead of making your own.*

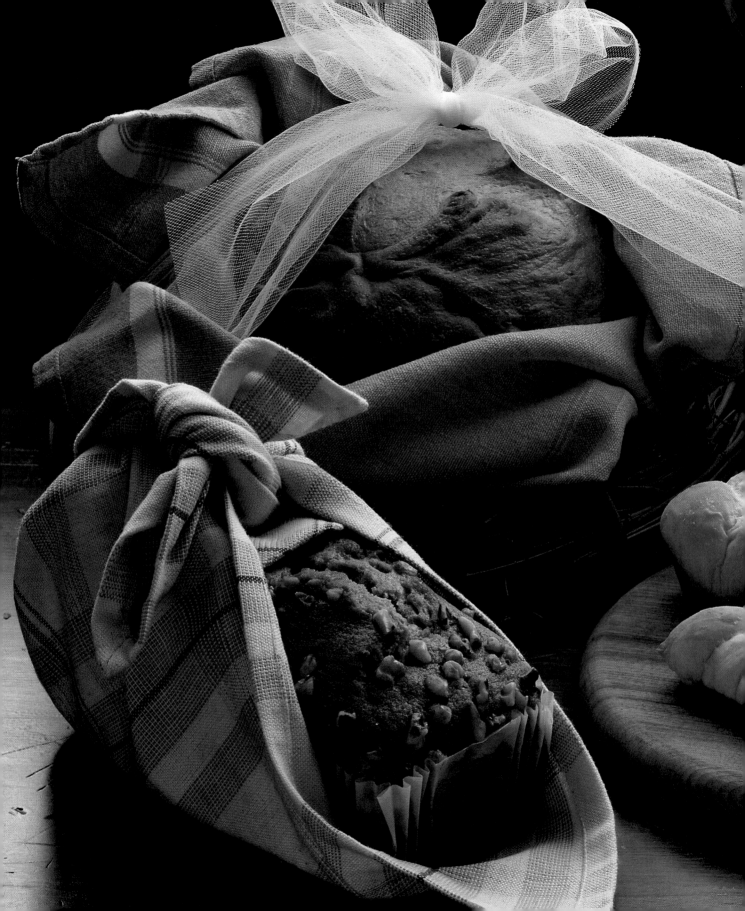

the *Bread* BASKET

Fresh bread or rolls make an ideal gift to take to a party or holiday dinner. Whether you bake your own bread or buy it at a bakery, you can present it with creative flair.

Wrap fresh rolls or muffins individually in cellophane tied with ribbon, and place them in vintage or new muffin tins. Wrap small quick-bread loaves in a linen towel or napkin. Or make a simple serving basket from a grapevine wreath lined with a linen napkin or towel. Leave the containers behind with your host as an additional gift.

If you want to make freshly baked bread or rolls, but don't have time for all the fuss, use frozen bread dough or a boxed hot roll mix. Follow package directions, shape the dough as desired, and bake it up fresh so it's ready to go when you are.

Linen–wrapped Bread

MATERIALS

❖Small loaf of bread, cooled ❖Square linen napkin or towel

☞ *Place wrapped loaf in a basket or shallow wooden bowl.*

1 Lay napkin on a flat surface with the corners pointing to the top and bottom. Fold top corner down two-thirds of the way to opposite corner.

2 Place loaf vertically on napkin near bottom corner so top edge can be folded over, covering two-thirds of loaf. Fold top edge over loaf.

3 Bring side corners of napkin together at top of bread, and tie in knot.

Grapevine wreath Basket

MATERIALS

❖Grapevine wreath, in desired size up to 12" (30.5 cm) diameter ❖Linen napkin or towel ❖Ribbon

1 Fold large pleat horizontally across napkin. Fold second large pleat vertically across napkin, so napkin fits across center of wreath with 1" to 2" (2.5 to 5 cm) overlap.

2 Line basket with folded napkin. Arrange rolls or bread in basket. Tie ribbon completely around basket and bread to secure.

Shaping Rolls from
Hot Roll Mix or Frozen Bread Dough

for 1 loaf (16 oz./453 g) frozen dough, defrosted,
or 1 box (16 oz./453 g) hot roll mix

Pan Rolls:

Roll 18 equal pieces of dough into balls, and place them evenly spaced in two greased 8" (20.5 cm) round baking pans.

Clovers:

Roll 18 equal pieces of dough into balls, and place them in 18 greased muffin tin cups. Let rise as directed. Just before baking, snip each ball in half, then in quarters, using scissors, cutting to bottom but not through ball.

Knots:

Roll 24 equal pieces of dough into 9" (23 cm) ropes. Tie a loose knot in center of each rope.

Twists:

Roll 24 equal pieces of dough into 12" (30.5 cm) ropes. Fold each rope in half, and twist three or four times. Pinch the ends to seal.

Cloverleaf Rolls:

Divide dough into 18 equal pieces. Divide each piece into three equal pieces; roll pieces into balls. Place three balls in each section of 18 greased muffin tin cups.

Note: Follow package directions for making of dough, rising, and final baking of bread.

GIFTS *of* Silver

A small gift made of sterling silver or silverplate is an elegant choice for the person who entertains in style. There are many items available at gift stores, housewares stores, and kitchen stores for reasonable prices.

Nice food-related items are tea caddies; serving pieces, such as spoons, forks, or pie servers; corkscrews; or a salt-and-pepper-shaker set. Tie these items with ribbons, or nestle them in gift boxes. Other simple gift items include photo frames, earrings or tie pins, ornaments, and even baskets in varying sizes. Fill the baskets with potpourri, dried flowers, or candy. Place a photo in the frame, if desired.

SEASONAL
Wreaths & swags

Present your host or hostess with a truly original gift—a wreath or swag decorated to suit the season. They are easy to make, and all the items you'll need are available at craft and hobby stores. Create the impact of a purchased wreath without the cost.

For a winter wreath, purchase a plain fresh or artificial pine wreath. Embellish it with pinecones, red berry stems, cinnamon sticks, and sleigh bells hung from red ribbon. In autumn, decorate a grapevine wreath with raffia, dried or silk flowers, autumn leaves, and a small basket or cornucopia filled with artificial fruit or dried or silk naturals. Spring and summer wreaths can be made with grapevine or straw wreaths covered with silk ivy and silk or dried flowers appropriate to the season.

Basic swags can be decorated in a similar fashion, using premade bundles of silk or dried flowers. Simple instructions and tips for assembling wreaths and swags are given on the following pages.

Tips for Embellishing Wreaths

MATERIALS

❖Wreath base, made from evergreen, grapevine, or straw ❖Ribbon
❖Desired embellishments, such as bells, dried naturals, pinecones,
fruit, or berries ❖22-gauge or 24-gauge paddle floral wire; wire
cutter ❖Floral tape, optional ❖Hot glue gun and glue sticks

☞ *Secure ribbon to wreath by weaving it through the wreath; create*

twists and turns in ribbon for depth. Secure as necessary with hot glue.

☞ *Make floral or berry
clusters by grouping items
together. Attach wire to
items as necessary. Wrap
stems and wires with
floral tape.*

☞ *Add wire along fragile stems of dried flowers
to strengthen them. Wrap stem and wire with
floral tape.*

☞ *Attach wire to embellishments like pinecones and cinnamon sticks. For a pinecone, wrap wire around bottom layers of cone; twist ends together and trim to 6" (15 cm) for attaching to wreath. For cinnamon stick, insert wire through length of the stick; wrap wire around stick, twisting end at the middle. Trim wire to 6" (15 cm) length.*

▶

☞ *Hang items like sleigh bells on wreaths by tying them at varying lengths with narrow ribbon or raffia.*

☞ *Anchor large embellishments such as a small basket or cornucopia to wreath, using wire. Lightweight items may be secured using hot glue.*

◀

☞ *Add luster to pinecones by applying aerosol antiquing stain in glossy wood tone. Gild other embellishments, such as twigs, pinecones, artichokes, fruit, or sprigs of greenery by applying gold aerosol acrylic paint.*

Seasonal Swags

MATERIALS

❖Long stems of silk or dried naturals, such as pine boughs, flowers, leaves ❖22-gauge or 24-gauge paddle floral wire and wire cutter, or rubber band ❖Pruning shears ❖Ribbon or raffia

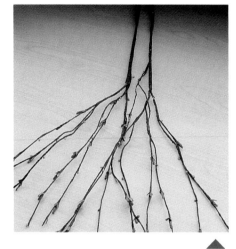

1 Place longest stems of the silk or dried naturals, such as leaves or other foliage, on flat surface; fan stems to create a base.

2 Place additional floral materials on top of the base, with stems at the same end. Trim additional stems so lengths of naturals are staggered and colors are balanced.

78

3 Secure ends of stems together, using floral wire or rubber band. Trim the ends of stems as desired, using pruning shears.

4 Cover wire or rubber band with ribbon or raffia tied in a bow.

☞ *For best results, use an odd number of floral materials. Choose three, five, seven, or nine items that coordinate.*

☞ *Add artificial berry clusters to fall or winter swags.*

☞ *For a Christmas swag, paint artificial pine boughs gold and burgundy with aerosol acrylic paint before constructing swag.*

Holiday
WREATHS
GARLANDS
& BOWS

9 Ft. Wired Garland Ribbon

HOLIDAY DECOR
Starter kit

If you have been invited to a housewarming party, consider giving first-time homeowners some holiday decorations for their new home. Present them with a collection of ready-made decorations or the necessary elements to create their own.

Fill a box with holiday decorating essentials, such as lights, ribbon, sets of ornaments, garland, candles and candle holders, and a holiday decorating book. A tree-starter kit could consist of a tree stand, plastic tree bag, a tree skirt, lights, and an extension cord.

If your gift recipient likes crafts, stop at a craft store and select an unadorned wreath, several yards of ribbon, berry stems, holiday bells, and a wreath-making book. Or purchase a gift certificate from the craft store along with a listing of holiday decorating classes.

new Homeowner GIFTS

New homeowners often lack many household essentials and are generally unfamiliar with their new neighborhood. At the housewarming party, give the new homeowners gifts they can really use.

Purchase a nice garbage pail or wicker wastepaper basket. Fill it with a welcome mat, brass house numbers, or an engraved door knocker, cleaning supplies, or light bulbs. In addition, include maps of the local area; lists of doctors, dentists, or hair salons; or gift certificates at nearby restaurants, decorating centers, or building supply stores.

Make a name plate or address signboard for display at the front door. Stencil the family name, paint simple designs, or attach wooden cutouts to an unfinished wooden sign, available at most hobby or craft stores.

Stenciled name Sign

MATERIALS

❖Unfinished wooden sign in desired size ❖Stencils for letters and other desired designs ❖Stencil tape ❖Craft acrylic paints ❖Disposable plates ❖Stencil brushes ❖Aerosol clear acrylic sealer

1 Secure stencil in desired position on sign, using stencil tape.

2 Pour paint of desired color onto disposable plate. Dip tip of stencil brush into paint. Using circular motion, blot brush onto folded paper towel until bristles are almost dry.

Address Signboard

MATERIALS

❖Unfinished wooden sign in desired size ❖Wooden letters and numbers ❖Wooden cutouts, if desired ❖Acrylic craft paints ❖Exterior wood glue ❖C-clamps, optional ❖Aerosol clear acrylic sealer

1 Paint sign, letters and numbers, and wooden cutouts in desired colors. Position letters, numbers, and cutouts on sign as desired.

3 Hold brush perpendicular to surface of stencil. As a test, blot brush on blank area of stencil plate, using a light circular stroke; if brush strokes are noticeable, blot the brush on paper towel again.

4 Hold the brush perpendicular to the surface of stencil, and apply paint, using a circular motion, within the cut areas of stencil. Allow to dry. Remove stencil. Repeat process with additional stencils and desired colors of paint until design is completed. Allow to dry.

5 Apply an even coat of aerosol acrylic sealer to sign. Allow to dry.

☞ *Instead of stenciling designs, use permanent opaque paint pens for lettering, or apply acrylic paint on signs with a fine liner brush.*

2 Secure the letters, numbers, and cutouts to sign, using wood glue. If desired, hold glued pieces in place with a C-clamp. Allow to dry.

3 Apply an even coat of aerosol acrylic sealer to the sign. Allow to dry.

SPRINGTIME
Gardener GIFTS

Early spring is the time of year when people begin to brush off winter's hold and start poring over the seed catalogs. If you know someone who eagerly waits for the frost to leave the ground, present that person with a selection of gardening goodies for your next gift-giving occasion.

Select a shallow basket with a handle—perfect for gathering flowers—and fill the basket with seed packets for flowers and herbs, a small bag of potting soil and peat pots, gardening gloves, a small trowel, and flower shears. Or wrap up a nice garden book; embellish the package with seed packets, or place a garden-center gift certificate inside the card.

OUTDOOR
Survival kits

Outdoor parties are favorite events throughout the summer. If you are invited to a beach party or picnic, go prepared with "survival kits" for your hosts.

Since outdoor picnics are magnets for bugs, fill a basket with citronella candles, a pleasant-smelling insect repellent, and a mesh food umbrella to cover open containers of food. Decorative tablecloth weights are also helpful to keep the picnic table covering from blowing away. If the picnic is held on or near Independence Day or Flag Day, add sparklers; miniature flags; streamers; and red, white and blue candles to the basket.

Beach parties are fun outings for young and old alike. Treat your host with a beach towel, sandals, and sunscreen placed in a beach bag. If there will be children at the party, fill a mesh bag with items to entertain them at the beach—such as pails and shovels, spray bottles, water guns, and a beach ball.

Woods-scent Pot
Stove top instructions: Sca
room by placi

STOVETOP
Potpourri

Prepare a simple potpourri blend and combine it with a decorative display bowl for an inexpensive gift. It is very easy to make the blends shown on the following pages, and only takes a little extra thought to present them nicely.

These blends can either be given in decorative microwaveproof bowls or in pretty jars or canisters if they are to be steeped on the stovetop. Include instructions for both uses.

Stovetop Potpourri

Woods-scent Potpourri

- ❖ 1/2 cup (125 mL) fresh pine needles
- ❖ 1/4 cup (50 mL) juniper berries
- ❖ 2 tablespoons (30 mL) dried rosemary leaves
- ❖ 1 tablespoon (15 mL) celery seed
- ❖ 1 tablespoon (15 mL) caraway seed
- ❖ 6 dried bay leaves, crumbled

Makes 1 cup (250 mL)

Instructions for Use

Stovetop instructions: *Scent room by placing 1 cup (250 mL) water and 1 tablespoon (15 mL) potpourri in small saucepan. Simmer over low heat for as long as desired.*

Microwave instructions: *Scent room by placing 1 cup (250 mL) hot water and 1 tablespoon (15 mL) potpourri in microwaveproof bowl. Microwave at High for 2 to 3 minutes, or until boiling. Place potpourri on coaster in desired room. When cool, microwave once or twice more.*

1 Combine all ingredients in a small plastic food-storage bag. Secure bag; shake to mix.

2 Place potpourri in decorative container with lid or in a cloth pouch, or simply leave potpourri in plastic bag. Tie pouch or bag shut with ribbon or raffia. If potpourri is left in bag, place bag in microwaveproof bowl with about 1-cup (250 mL) capacity. Include a decorative label or card with instructions for use, left. ▼

Citrus-Spice Potpourri

- 1 orange
- 1 lemon
- 1 lime
- 1/3 cup (75 mL) water
- 1/4 cup (50 mL) whole cloves
- 2 tablespoons (30 mL) whole allspice
- 3 sticks cinnamon, broken up
- 4 dried bay leaves, crumbled

Makes 1 cup (250 mL)

1 Cut long strips of peel from orange, lemon, and lime, using a vegetable peeler or sharp knife; be careful not to remove white membrane. Cut strips into 1" (2.5 cm) lengths. Reserve fruit for other uses.

2 Arrange peels in single layer on paper-towel-lined plate. Place water in 1-cup (250 mL) measure. Place water and plate in microwave oven. Microwave at High for 4 to 5 minutes, or just until peels begin to dry, tossing with fingers after every minute. Arrange peels on second paper towel; allow peels to air dry for 24 hours.

3 Continue as directed in steps 1 and 2, for *Woods-scent Potpourri,* opposite.

INDEX

A

Address signboard for new
 homeowners, 83-85

B

Bags, wine-bottle, 41-42
Baskets,
 bread, 69-71
 breakfast Easter, 65-67
Bells, dinner, 19
Birch-log gifts, 39
Bobèches, 25-27
Books, 53
Boxes, decorating, 35-36
Bread basket, 69-71
Breakfast Easter basket, 65-67

C

Candles,
 bobèches for, 25-27
 votive, 21-23
Candy and snack presentations, 35-37
Casseroles, 33
Cassette tapes, customized, 59
 covers and labels, 60-61
Cellophane and tissue wrap for fresh
 flowers, 6-7
Cider, mulled, 45-46
Coasters, homemade, 49-51
Containers,
 bread basket, 69-71
 breakfast Easter basket, 65-67
 for flowers and plants, 5
 wine-bottle, 41-43
Covers for cassette tapes, 59-61
Crystal and glass gifts, 9
Customized music tapes, 59-61

D

Day-after party gift, 63
Dinner bells, 19
Dipped pretzels, in bundles, 35, 37
Dispensers, drink, 33
Dried flowers, 5
 on wreaths and swags, 75-79
Dried fruit, 29
Drinks,
 coasters, 49-51
 dispensers, 33
 hot mulled, 45-47

E

Easter basket, breakfast, 65-67

F

Flower and plant presentations,
 dried, 5, 75-79
 fresh, 5-7
Folding techniques for table linens,
 15-17
Food gifts,
 bread basket, 69-71
 breakfast Easter basket, 65-67
 candy and snack presentations, 35-37
 fruits and nuts, 29-31
 potluck, 33
Fresh flowers, 5-7
Fruit, dried, 29

G

Gardener gifts, 87
Glass and crystal gifts, 9
Grapevine wreath bread basket, 69-70

H

Holiday decor starter kit, 81
Hot mulled drinks, 45-47
Housewarming gifts, 81, 83-85

K

Knotted rope napkin rings, 11, 13

L

Labels for cassette tapes, 59-61
Linens, folded as bouquets, 15-17

M

Mixed nuts, recipe for, 31
Mulled drinks, hot, 45-47
Music tapes, customized, 59-61

N

Name sign, stenciled, for new
 homeowners, 83-85
Napkin rings, 11-13
Napkins, 11, 15-17
New homeowner gifts, 83-85
Nuts, 29
 nut pot, 30
 spicy mixed, 31

O

Outdoor parties, survival kits for, 89

P

Personalized stationery, 55-57
Plant and flower presentations, 5-7
Potluck gifts, 33
Potpourri, stovetop, 91-93
Pretzels, dipped, in bundles, 35, 37

R

Recipes,
  dipped pretzel rods, 37
  hot mulled drinks, 46-47
  spicy mixed nuts, 31
  stovetop potpourri, 92-93
  trail mix, 31
Rings, napkin, 11-13
Rolls, shaped from hot roll mix or
  frozen bread dough, 71
Rope napkin rings, knotted, 11, 13

S

Seasonal wreaths and swags, 75-79
Silver gifts, 73
Snack and candy presentations, 35-37
Springtime gardener gifts, 87
Stamping techniques and tips, 56-57
Starter kit, holiday decor, 81
Stationery, personalized, 55-57
Stenciled name sign for new
  homeowners, 83-85
Sterling silver gifts, 73
Stovetop potpourri, 91-93
Survival kits for outdoor parties, 89
Swags and wreaths, seasonal, 75-79

T

Table linen bouquets, 15-17
Tapes, music, customized, 59-61
Tissue and cellophane wrap for fresh
  flowers, 6-7
Towels, folded as bouquets, 15-17
Trail mix, 29, 31

V

Votive candles, 21-23

W

Wassail, 45
  recipe for, 47
Wine, mulled, 45
  recipe for, 47
Wine-bottle bags and containers,
  41-43
Wire napkin rings, 11-13
Wrapping fresh flowers, 6-7
Wreaths,
  grapevine, as bread basket, 69-70
  seasonal, 75-79

CREDITS

CY DECOSSE INCORPORATED

A COWLES MAGAZINES COMPANY

Chairman/CEO: Bruce Barnet
Chairman Emeritus: Cy DeCosse
President/COO: Nino Tarantino
Executive V.P./Editor-in-Chief:
  William B. Jones

TOAST THE HOST
Created by: The Editors of
  Cy DeCosse Incorporated

Also available from the publisher:
*Grand Slam Gifts, Greet the Season,
Wrap It Up*

Group Executive Editor: Zoe A. Graul
Editorial Manager: Dawn M. Anderson
Senior Editor/Writer: Ellen C. Boeke
Project Manager: Amy Berndt

Associate Creative Director: Lisa Rosenthal
Art Director: Stephanie Michaud
Editor: Janice Cauley
Researchers/Designers: Michael Basler,
  Christine Jahns
Sample Production Manager: Carol Olson
Technical Photo Stylists: Bridget Haugh,
  Sue Jorgensen, Nancy Sundeen
Styling Director: Bobbette Destiche
Project Stylists: Christine Jahns,
  Joanne Wawra
Prop Stylists: Elizabeth Emmons,
  Michele Joy
Food Stylists: Elizabeth Emmons,
  Nancy Johnson
Artisans: Arlene Dohrman,
  Phyllis Galbraith, Valerie Hill,
  Kristi Kuhnau, Virginia Mateen,
  Carol Pilot, Michelle Skudlarek
Vice President of Photography & Production:
  Jim Bindas
Director of Photography: Mike Parker
Creative Photo Coordinator: Cathleen Shannon
Studio Manager: Marcia Chambers
Lead Photographer: Rebecca Schmitt
Photographer: William Lindner
Contributing Photographer: Steve Smith

Print Production Manager: Patt Sizer
Desktop Publishing Specialist:
  Laurie Kristensen
Production Staff: Laura Hokkanen,
  Tom Hoops, Jeanette Moss, Mike Schauer,
  Michael Sipe, Brent Thomas, Greg Wallace,
  Kay Wethern
Shop Supervisor: Phil Juntti
Scenic Carpenters: Troy Johnson,
  Rob Johnstone, John Nadeau
Contributors: Design Master; Duff Associates;
  Honey Wax; Plaid Enterprises
Sources for Product Information:
  Candy coating—Sweet Celebrations,
  P.O. Box 39426, Edina, MN 55439,
  (800) 328-6722
Printed on American paper by:
  R. R. Donnelley & Sons Co. (0796)
99 98 97 96 / 5 4 3 2 1

Cy DeCosse Incorporated offers
a variety of how-to books. For
information write:
  Cy DeCosse Subscriber Books
  5900 Green Oak Drive
  Minnetonka, MN 55343